Cassia Harvey

Serial Shifting

Exercises for the Cello

Part One: 1st to 4th Position.....Page 3
Part Two: 1st to 8th Position.....Page 16

CHPD106

©2001, 2016 by C. Harvey Publications All Rights Reserved.

www.charveypublications.com - print books
www.learnstrings.com - PDF downloadable books
www.harveystringarrangements.com - chamber music

Serial Shifting: Exercises for the Cello

Part One: 1st to 4th Position

1
1st finger to 1st finger shifting

I = A String
II = D String
III = G String
IV = C String

2
1st finger to 1st finger shifting

©2001 C. Harvey Publications All Rights Reserved.

3
1st finger to 1st finger shifting

4
1st finger to 1st finger shifting

7

2nd finger and 3rd finger shifting

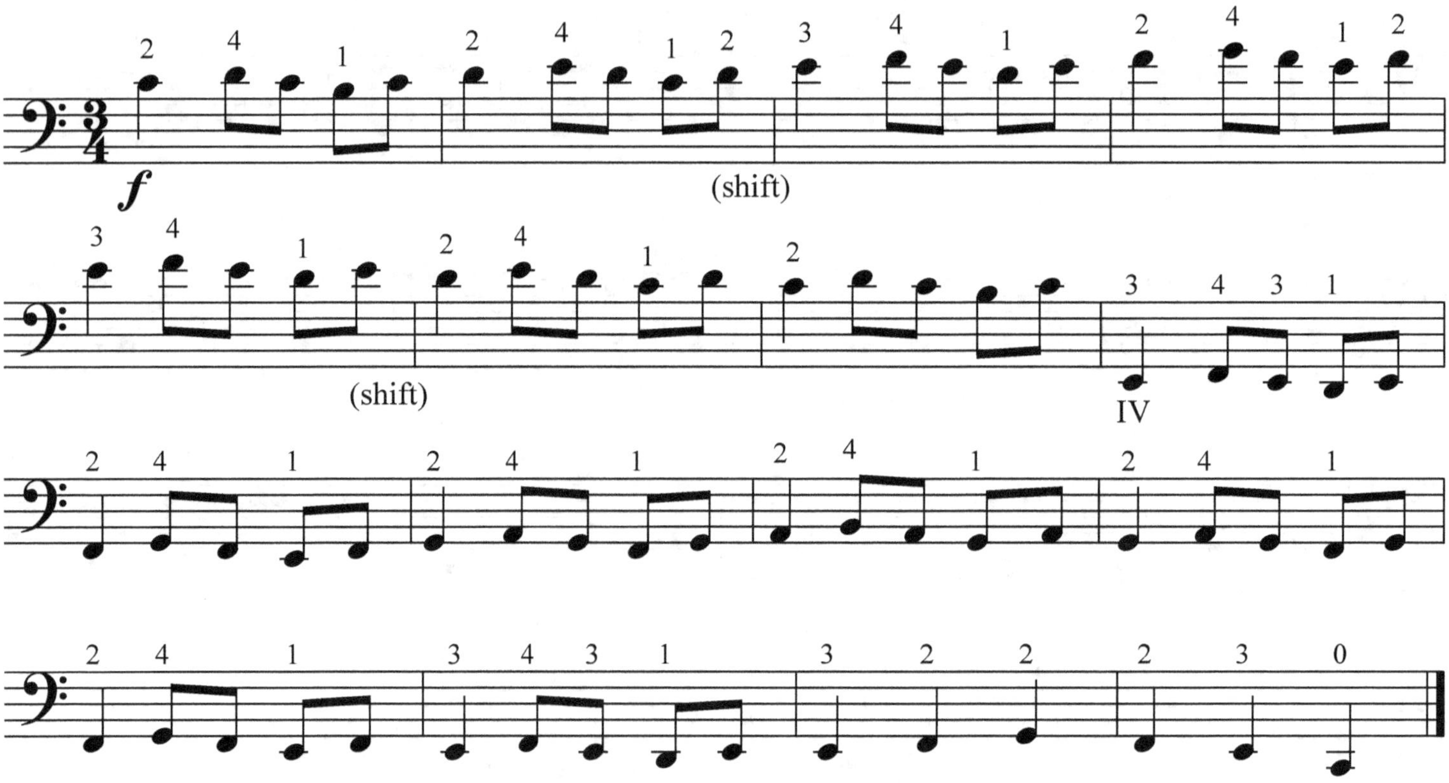

8

2nd finger and 3rd finger shifting

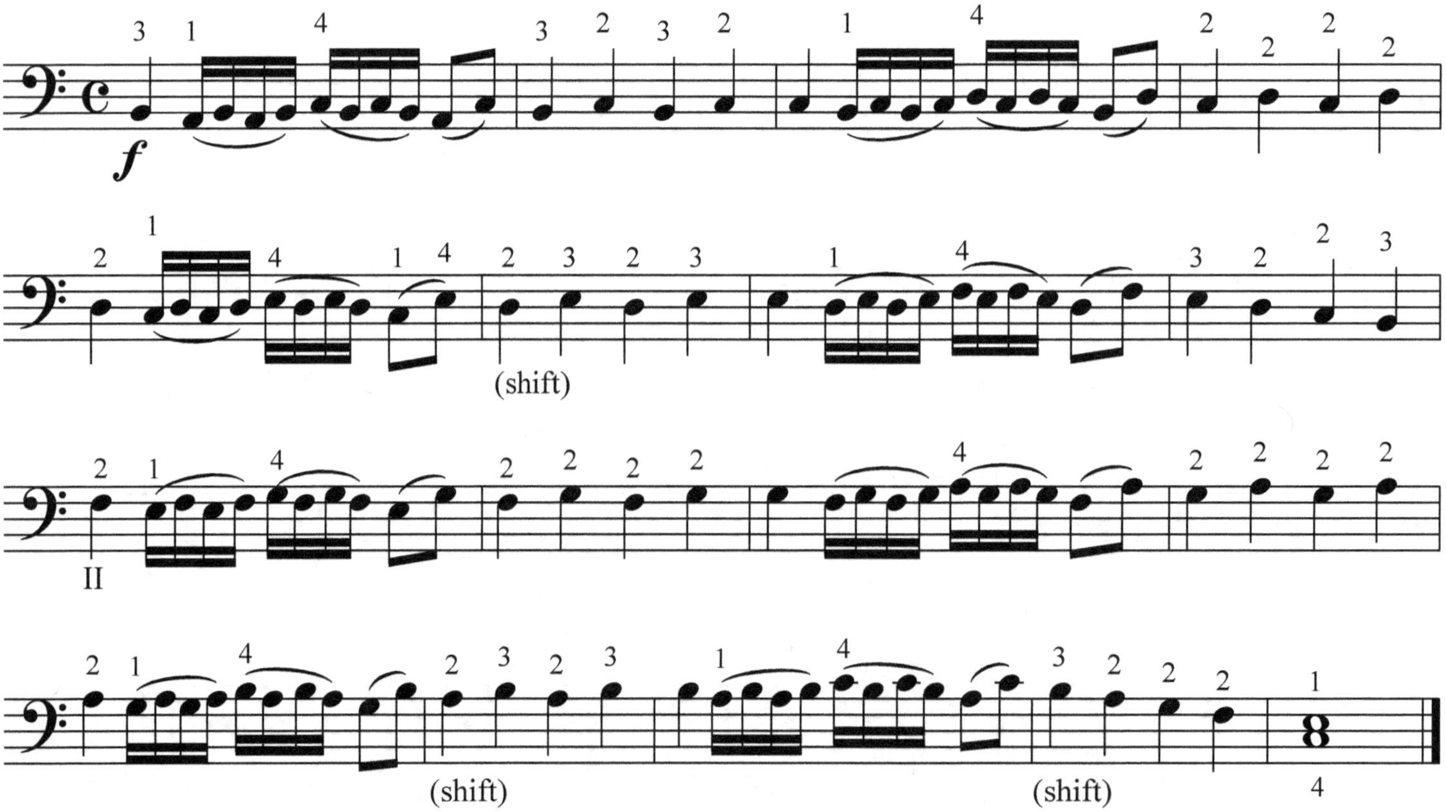

Serial Shifting; Exercises for the Cello

9
4th finger to 4th finger shifting

10
4th finger to 4th finger shifting

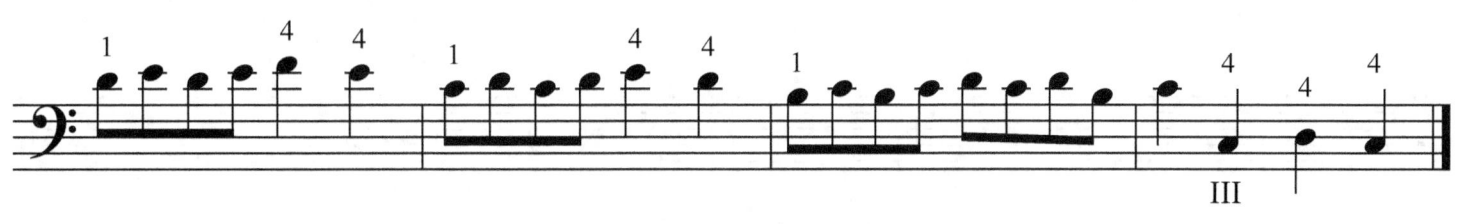

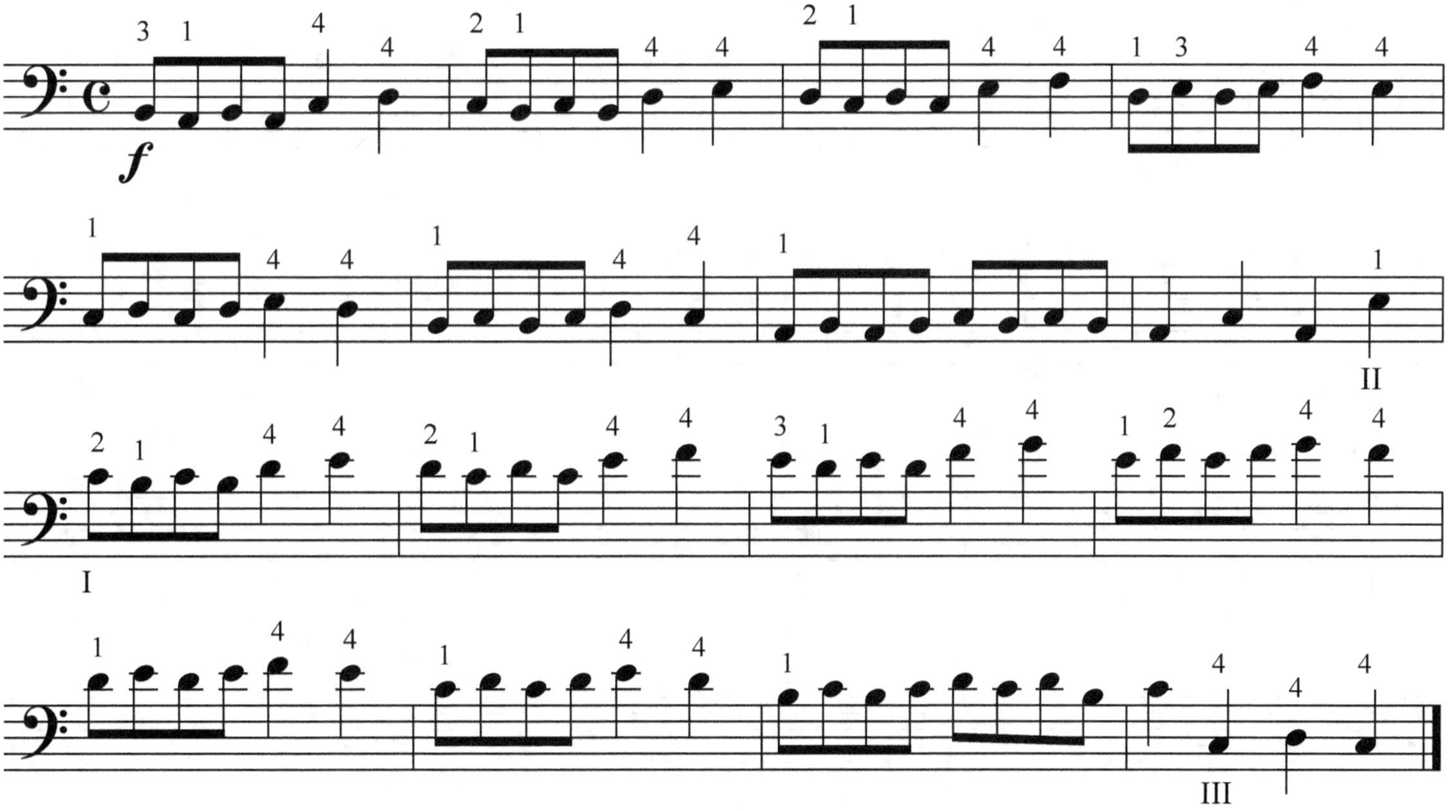

11

4th finger to 4th finger shifting

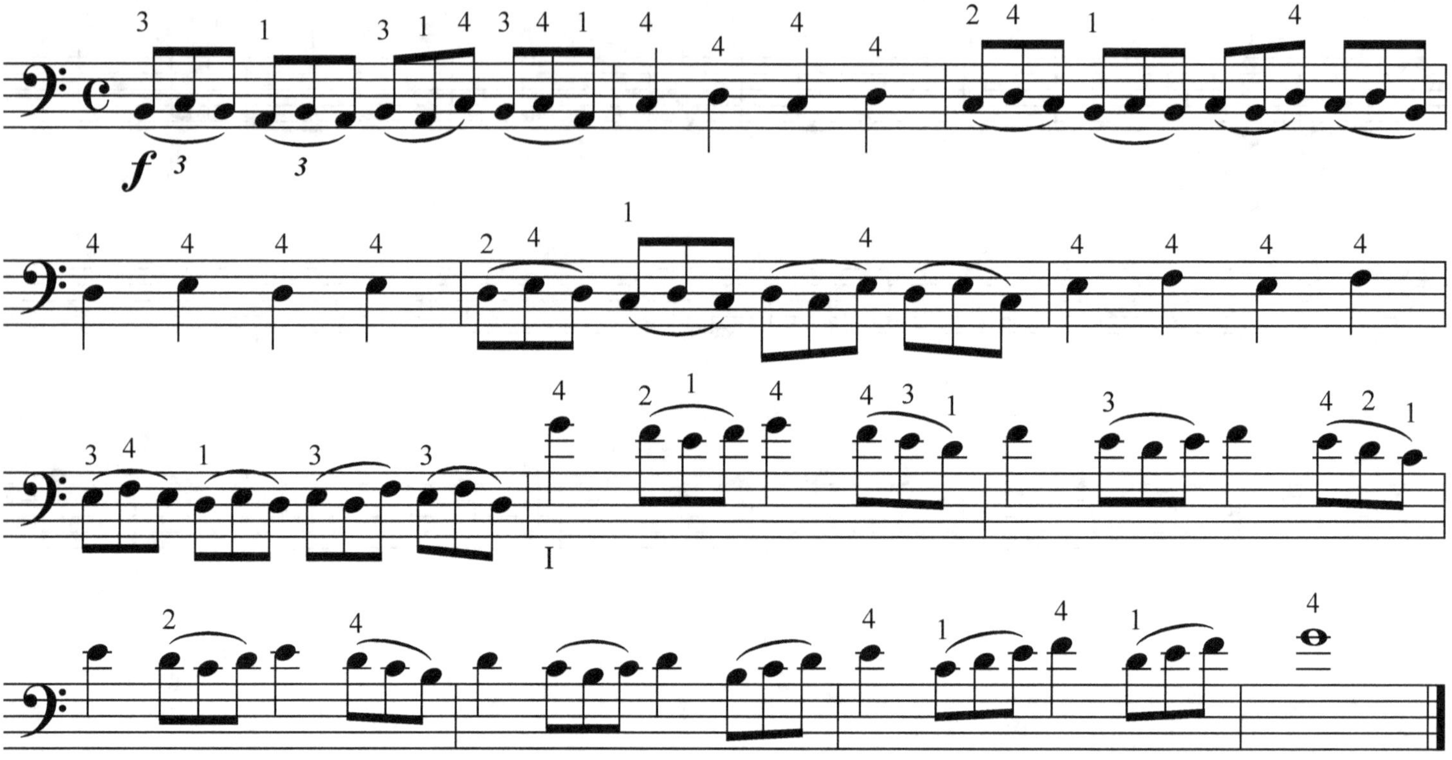

12

Substitution shifting

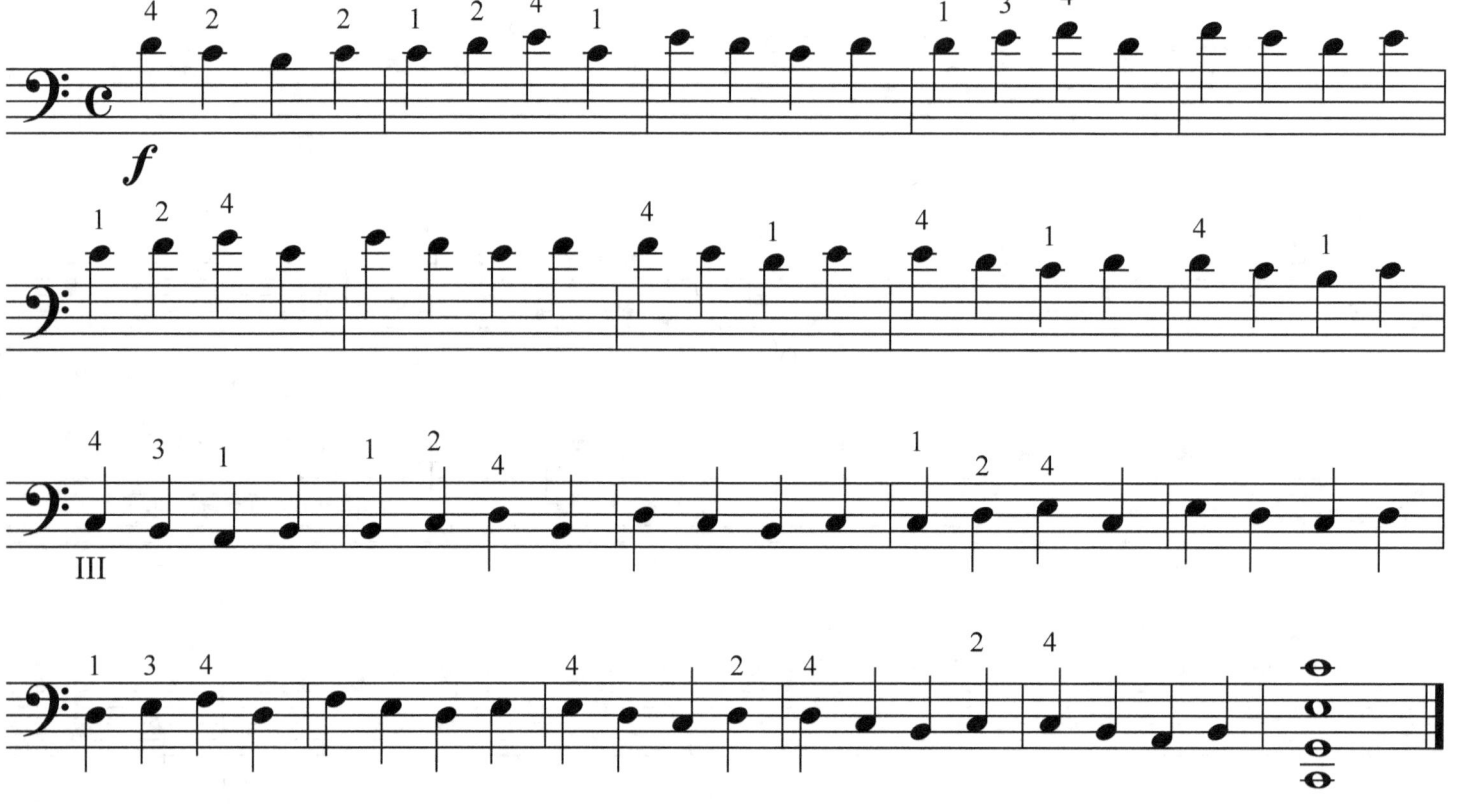

Serial Shifting; Exercises for the Cello

17
'Same-finger' shifting and substitution shifting

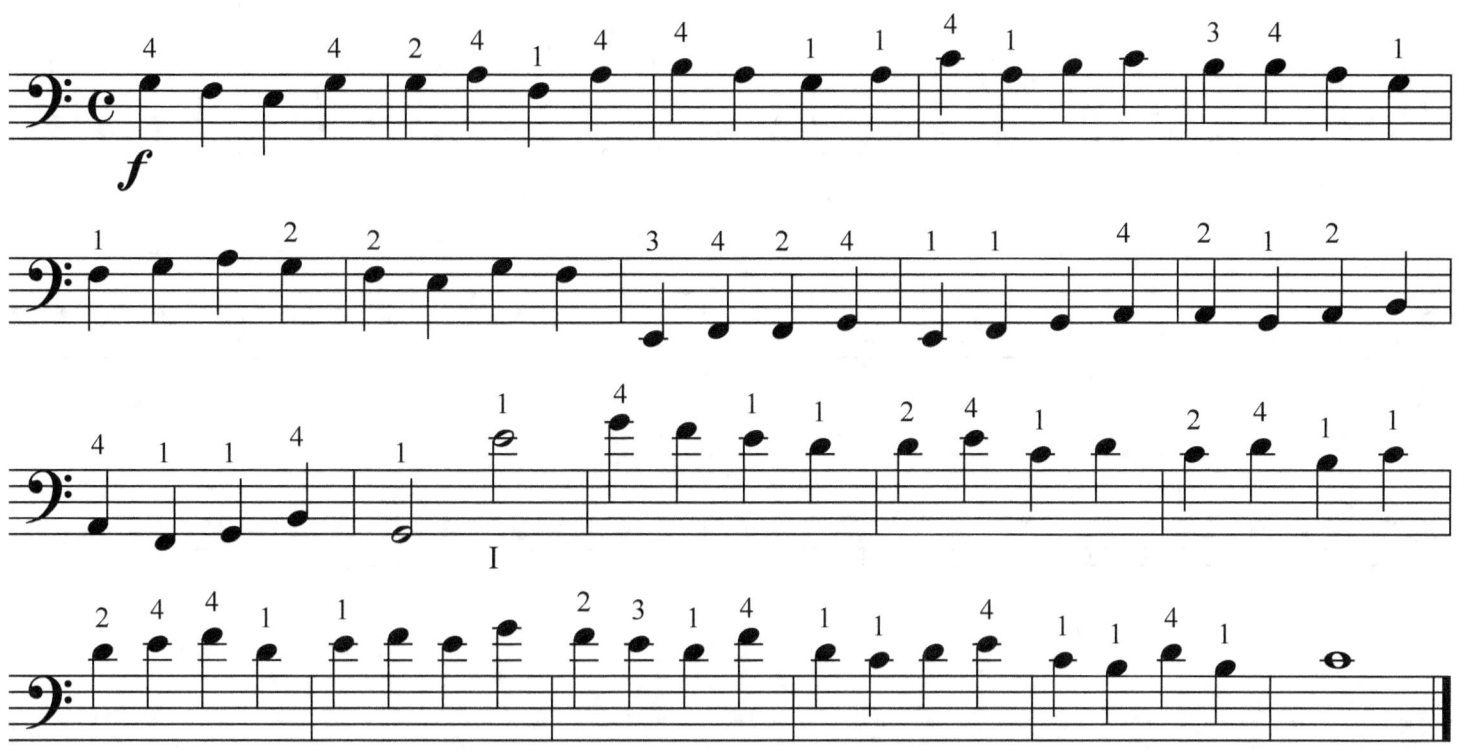

'Creeping' is shifting where one finger is held down on the string and another finger is moved into place below or above it. Holding 4th finger down, slide/lift 1st finger up to where 2nd finger was. Lift middle two fingers to give 1st finger freedom to move. Then lift 4th finger and play to see if 1st finger has been moved to the correct place.

18
'Creeping'

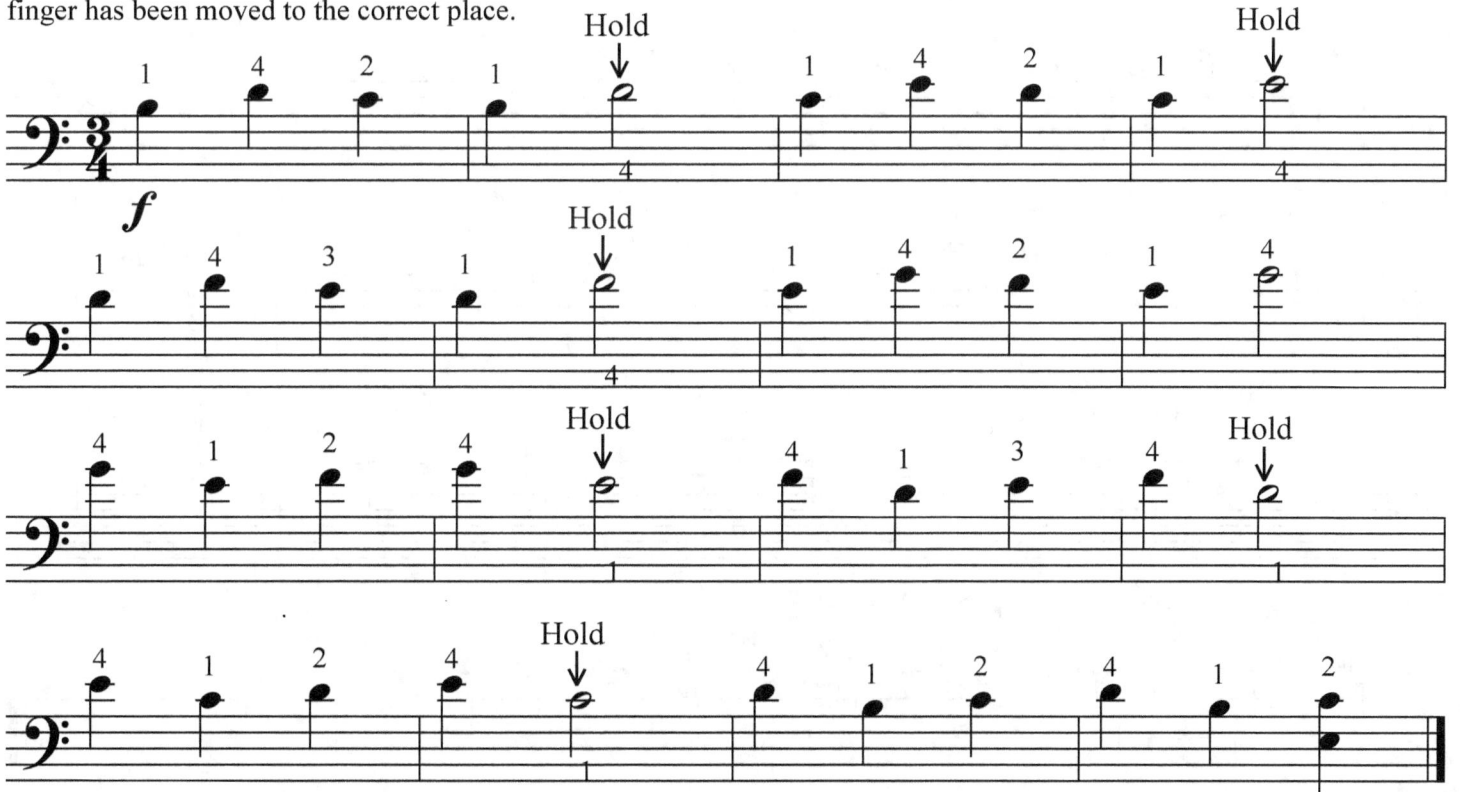

©2001 C. Harvey Publications All Rights Reserved.

19

'Creeping'

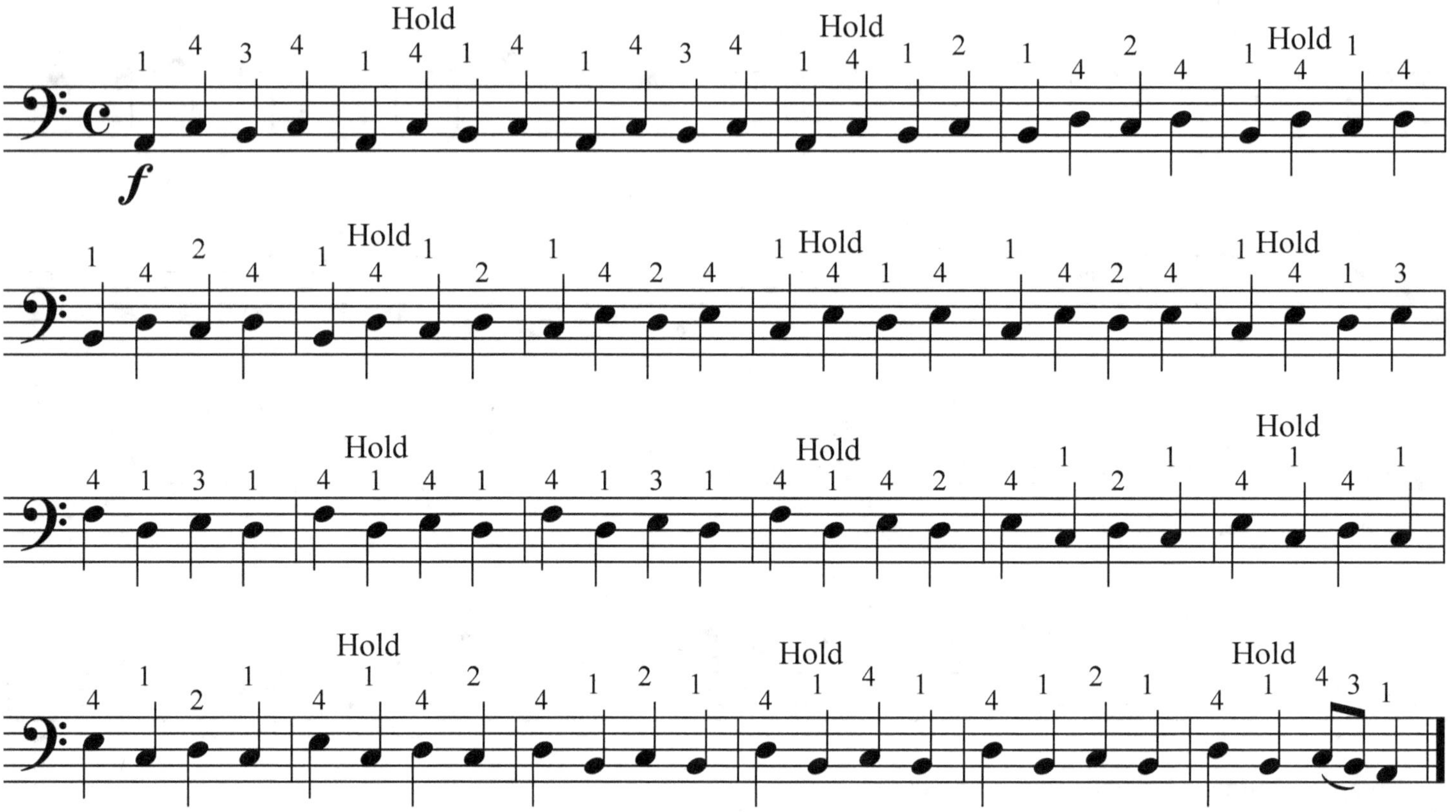

20

'Creeping'

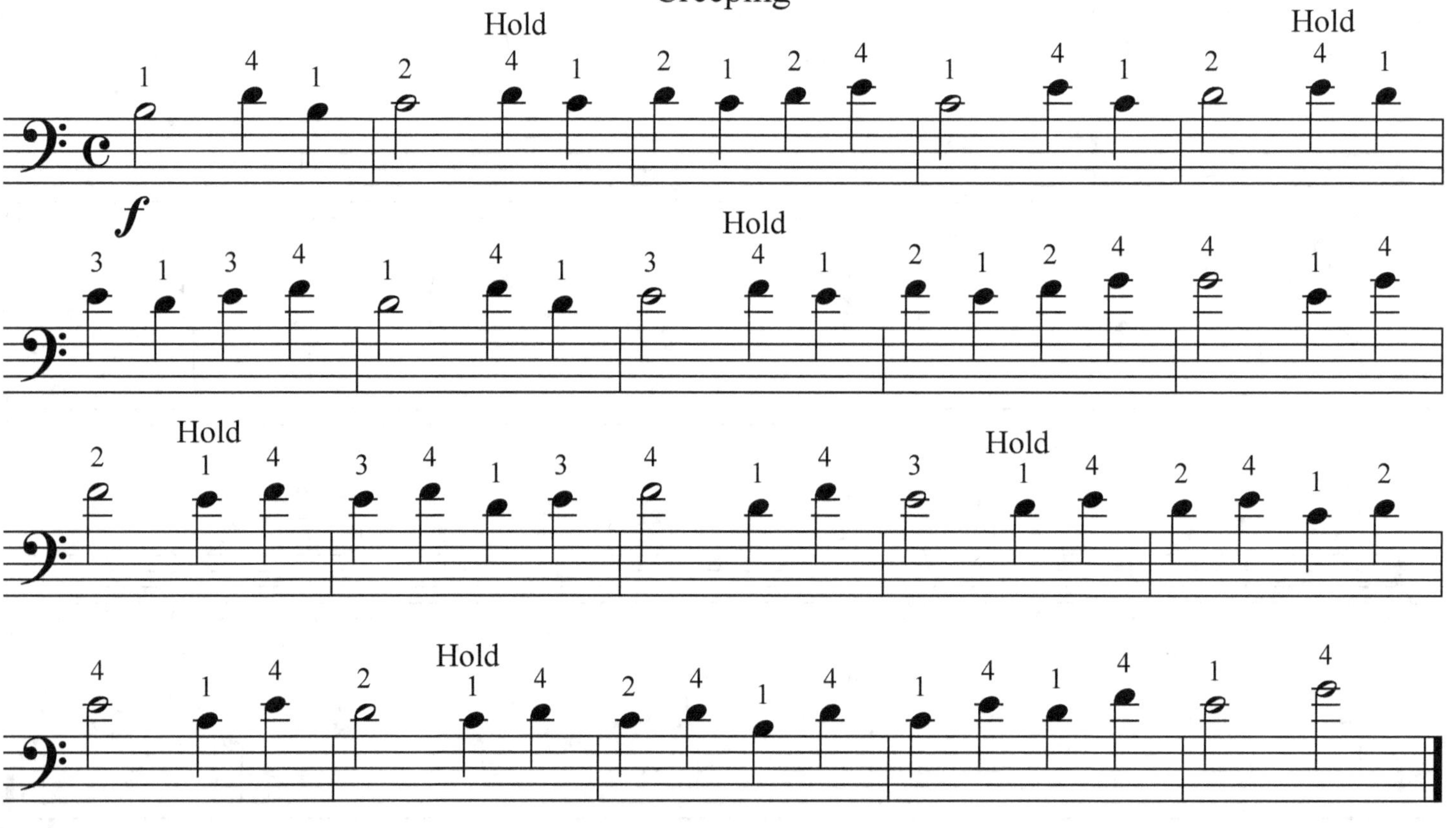

Serial Shifting; Exercises for the Cello

©2001 C. Harvey Publications All Rights Reserved.

23
'Creeping'

24
'Same-finger' shifting, substitution shifting, and 'creeping'

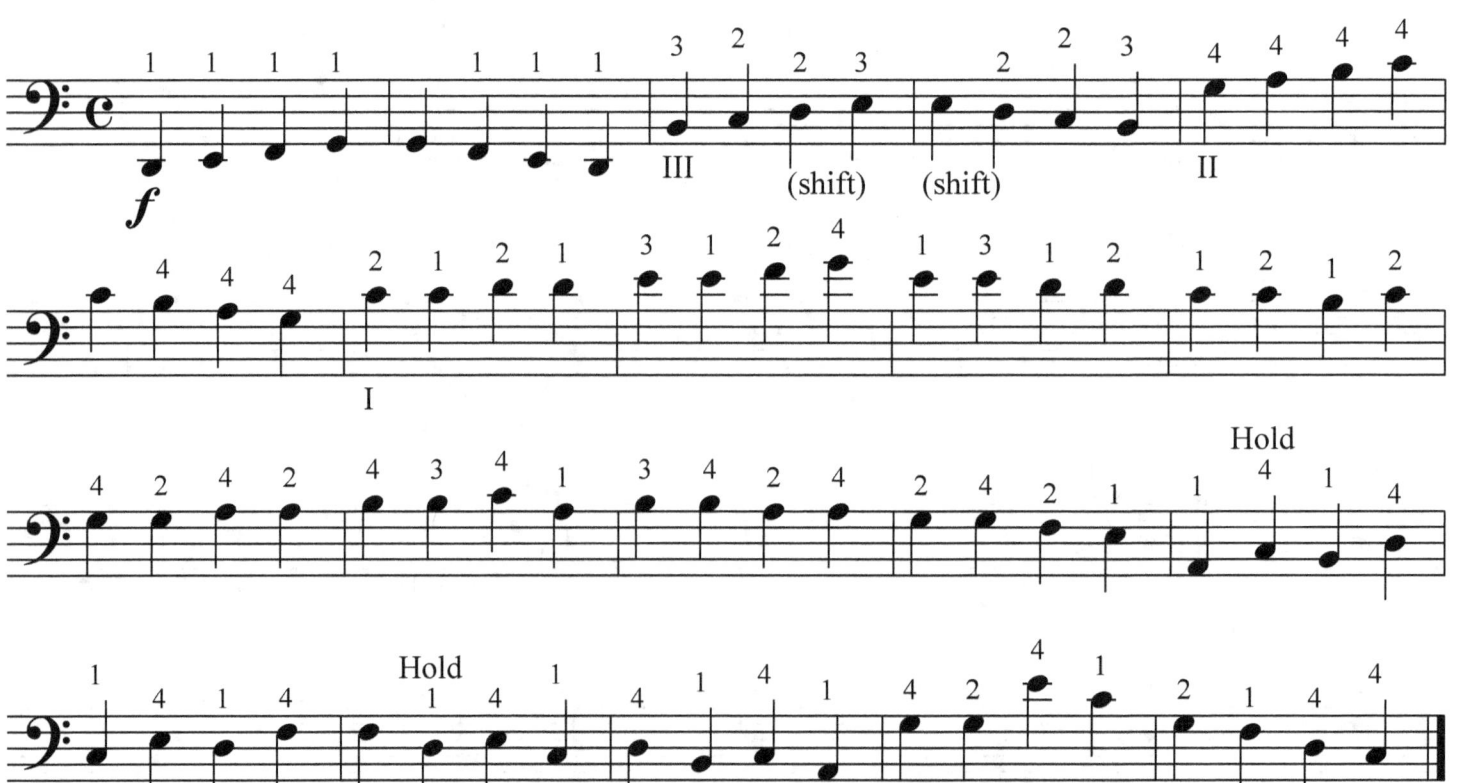

25
'Same-finger' shifting, substitution shifting, and 'creeping'

Part Two: 1st to 8th Position

26

1st finger to 1st finger shifting

Stay on the D string for this exercise.

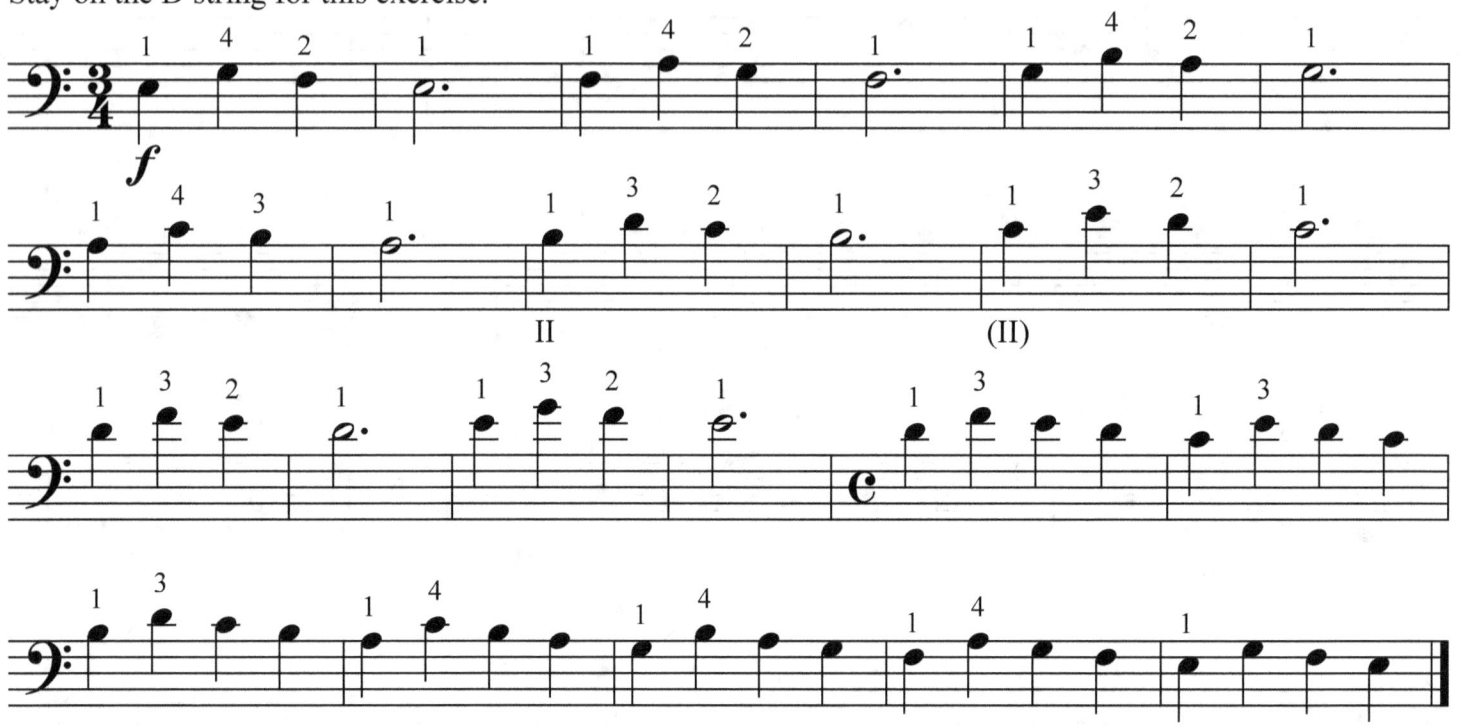

27

1st finger to 1st finger shifting

Stay on the G string for this exercise.

©2001 C. Harvey Publications All Rights Reserved.

28
1st finger to 1st finger shifting

29

1st finger to 1st finger shifting

Stay on the C string for this exercise.

30
1st finger to 1st finger shifting

Stay on the G string for this exercise.

31
2nd finger and 3rd finger shifting

Stay on the D string for this exercise.

32
2nd finger and 3rd finger shifting

33

2nd finger and 3rd finger shifting

Stay on the G string for this exercise.

34
3rd finger and 4th finger shifting

Stay on the C string for this exercise.

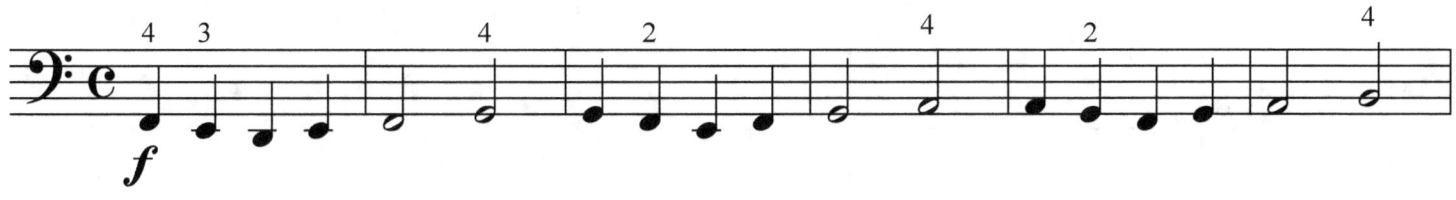

35
3rd finger and 4th finger shifting

Stay on the G string for this exercise.

36

3rd finger and 4th finger shifting

Stay on the G string for the first five lines.

37
Substitution shifting

38
Substitution shifting

Stay on the C string for this exercise.

39
Substitution shifting

Stay on the D string for this exercise.

40
Substitution shifting

Stay on the A string for this exercise.

Serial Shifting; Exercises for the Cello 29

41
Substitution shifting

This exercise alternates between the D and G strings.

©2001 C. Harvey Publications All Rights Reserved.

42
'Same-finger' shifting and substitution shifting

43
'Creeping'

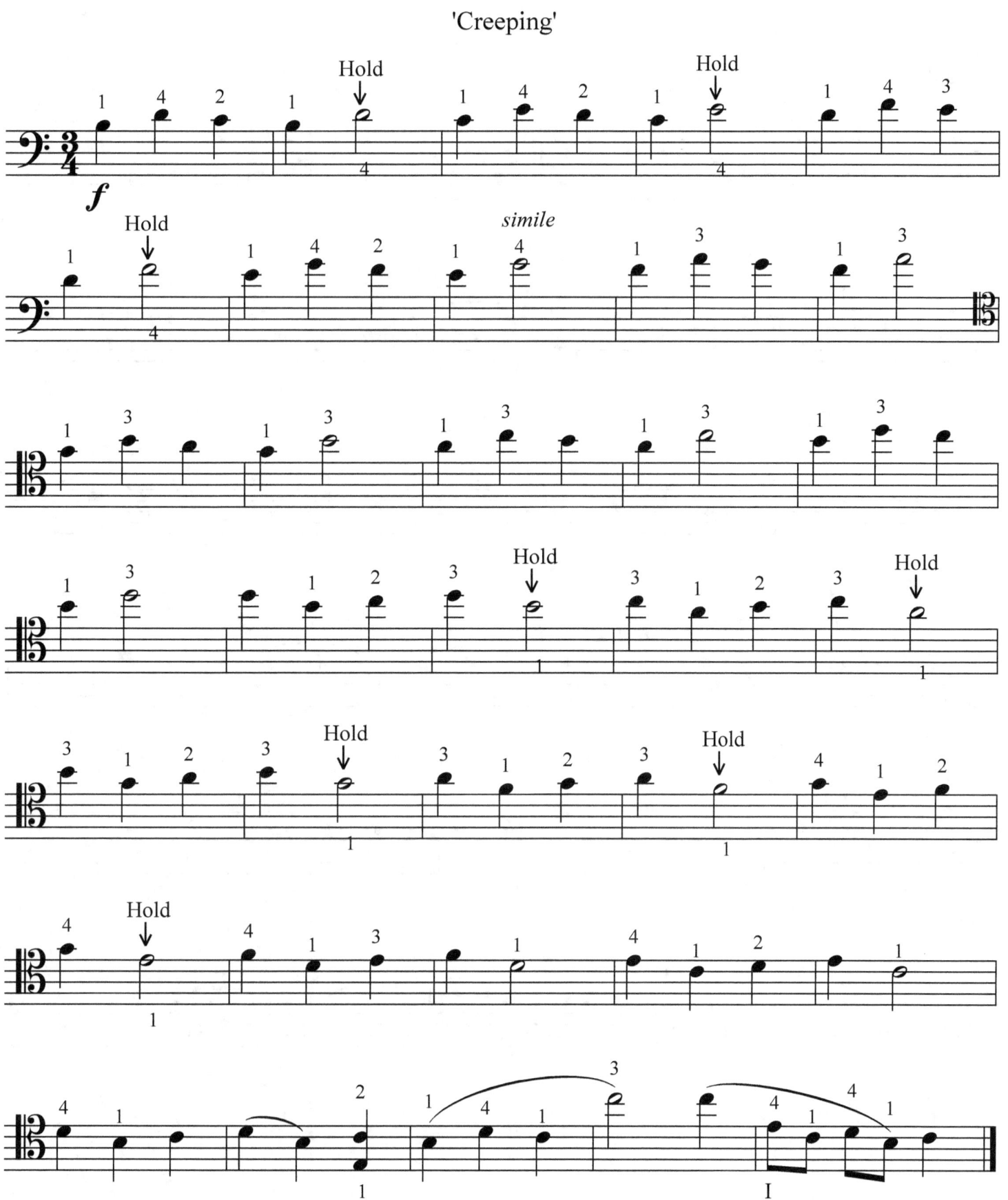

44
'Creeping'

Stay on the G string for this exercise.

45
'Creeping'

46
'Creeping'

Stay on the D string for this exercise.

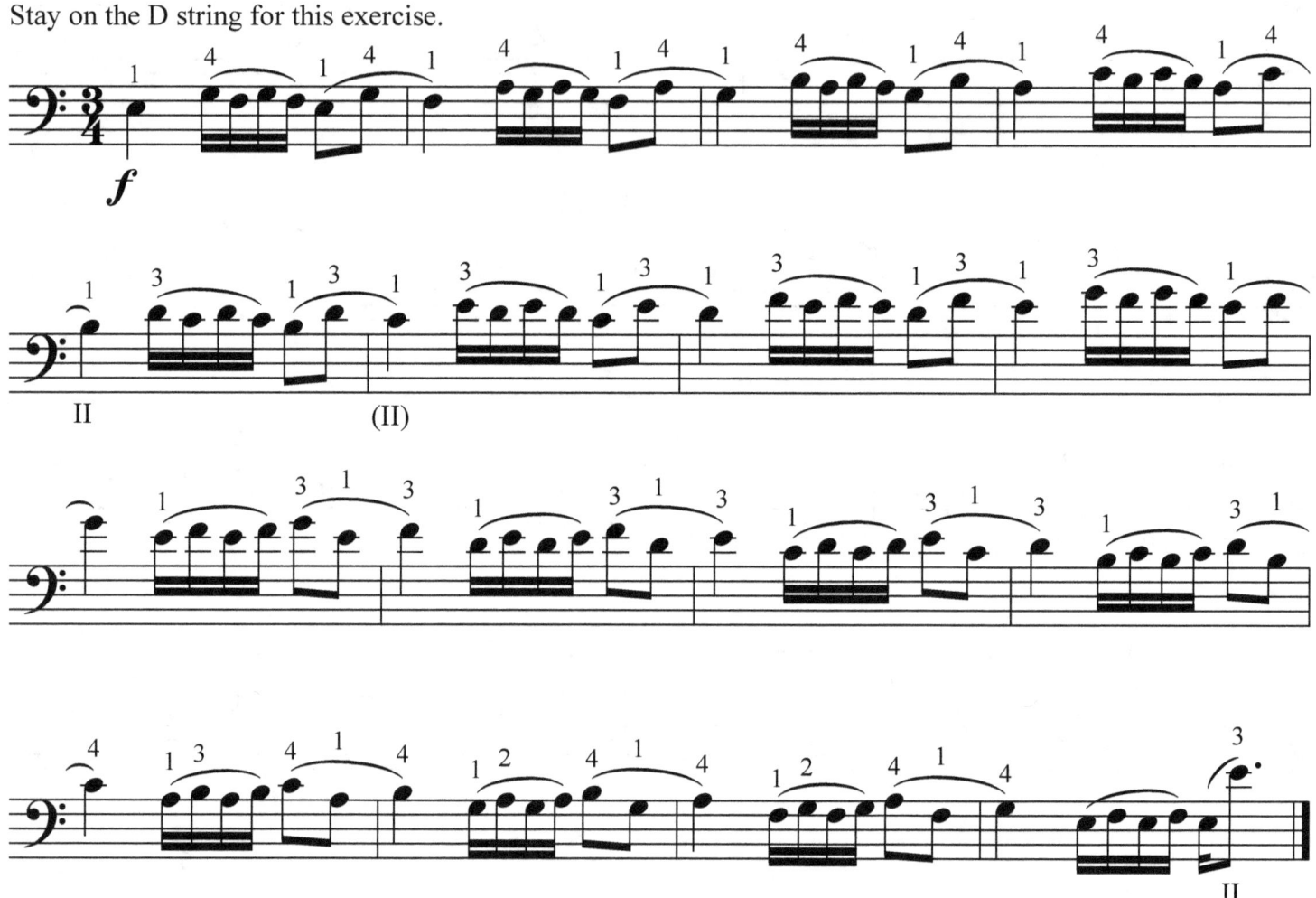

47
'Creeping'

Stay on the C string for this exercise.

48
'Creeping'

Stay on the G string for this exercise.

49
'Same-finger' shifting, substitution shifting, and 'creeping'

50
'Same-finger' shifting, substitution shifting, and 'creeping'

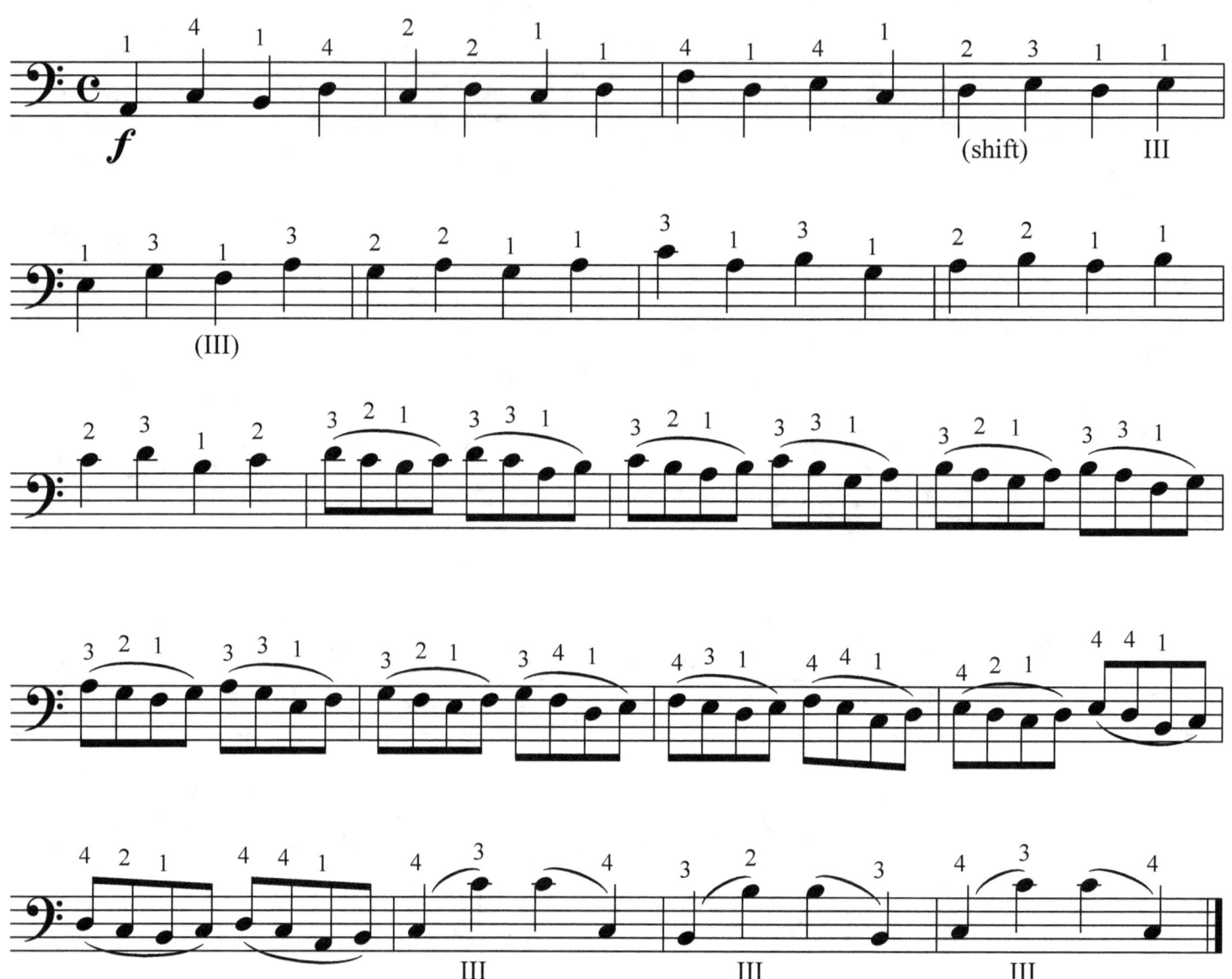

available from www.charveypublications.com: CHP244

Shifting in Keys for Cello, Book One

C Major Study No. 1

©2014 C. Harvey Publications All Rights Reserved.

www.ingramcontent.com/pod-product-compliance
Lightning Source LLC
Chambersburg PA
CBHW051427070526
44584CB00023B/3611